NATURE IN FOCUS

LIFE IN A RAIN FOREST

By Lorien Kite

Please visit our Web site www.garethstevens.com. For a free color catalog of all our high-quality books, call toll free 1-800-542-2595 or fax 1-877-542-2596.

Library of Congress Cataloging-in-Publication Data
Kite, Lorien.
    Life in a rain forest / Lorien Kite.
       p. cm. — (Nature in focus)
    Includes index.
    ISBN 978-1-4339-3410-0 (library binding) — ISBN 978-1-4339-3408-7 (pbk.)
    ISBN 978-1-4339-3409-4 (6-pack)
    1. Rain forest ecology—Juvenile literature. 2. Rain forests—Juvenile literature. I. Title.
    QH86.K53 2010
    578.734—dc22   2009037190

Published in 2010 by
Gareth Stevens Publishing
111 East 14th Street, Suite 349
New York, NY 10003

© 2010 The Brown Reference Group Ltd.

For Gareth Stevens Publishing:
Art Direction: Haley Harasymiw
Editorial Direction: Kerri O'Donnell

For The Brown Reference Group Ltd:
Editorial Director: Lindsey Lowe
Managing Editor: Tim Harris
Editor: Jolyon Goddard
Children's Publisher: Anne O'Daly
Design Manager: David Poole
Designer: Lorna Phillips
Picture Manager: Sophie Mortimer
Picture Researcher: Clare Newman
Production Director: Alastair Gourlay

Picture Credits:
Front Cover: Shutterstock: Fedor Selivanov (main image); Wong Yu Liang (background)
FLPA: Foto Natura/Minden Pictures: 23b, 29; ImageBroker: 22; Frans Lanting: 28; Thomas Marent: 21 inset; Chris mattison: 24; Terry Whittaker: 25; istockphoto: 5, 7b, 13b, 27; Shutterstock: 3, 7c; John Arnold: 23t; Mircea Bezergheanu: 30; Sascha Burkard: 17; Craig Dingle: 12; Karel Gallas: 20; Joe Gough: 8; Cynthia Kidwell: 7t; Gaham S. Klotz: 10-11; Wong Yu Liang: 19; OpenBest Designstock: 14; Lee Prince: 11b; Dr. Morley Read: 13t, 18, 21, 26; Jamie Robinson: 16; Desiree Walstra: 31; World Wildlife Wonders: 11b
All Artworks Brown Reference Group

All rights reserved. No part of this book may be reproduced in any form without permission in writing from the publisher, except by a reviewer.

Manufactured in the United States of America
1 2 3 4 5 6 7 8 9   12 11 10

CPSIA compliance information: Batch #BRW0102GS: For further information contact Gareth Stevens, New York, New York at 1-800-542-2595.

Contents

Rain Forests of the World	4
Life in a Rain Forest Tree	6
Life in the Canopy	8
Understory Life	18
Life on the Forest Floor	24
Life in a Tree Near You	30
Glossary	32
Index	32

Rain Forests of the World

Tropical rain forests grow where it is warm and wet all year round. They are home to more living things than any other habitat on Earth. This book introduces the plants and animals that live in a South American rain forest. You will see how they depend on one another and how each plays its part in the life of the forest.

The tropical rain forests of the world are shown in red on this world map.

A tropical rain forest is hot and steamy.

Many animals, including monkeys, parrots, wild cats, big snakes, and beautiful butterflies live deep inside the forest.

Life in a Rain Forest Tree

Tropical rain forests are home to more than half of all the kinds of plants and animals on Earth. Rain forest trees can be more than 200 feet (61 m) tall. They divide into layers, like the stories of a building. The top branches get a lot of sunshine. The layers get darker as you go down. Different plants and animals live in each layer.

The Amazon rain forest (in red) is in South America.

LIFE IN THE CANOPY

The canopy is where the trees spread their branches to form a crowded, leafy roof over the forest. Many animals live and feed there, including sloths, monkeys, brightly colored birds, butterflies and other insects, tree frogs, and lizards.

UNDERSTORY LIFE

The leaves of the canopy shade the understory from the Sun. There, straight, branchless trunks tower up toward the light. Orchids, tree ferns, snakes, and anteaters are all found in the understory.

LIFE ON THE FOREST FLOOR

Little light reaches the forest floor. This is the gloomiest part of the forest. Fungi grow in the damp darkness. Animals of the forest floor include jaguars, tapirs, and peccaries. Forest peoples can be found there, too.

Life in the Canopy

The canopy is the level where the treetops join together. There, the giant rain forest trees unfurl their leaves to soak up sunshine. Trees need the Sun's energy to make leaves and seeds. Some trees even turn their leaves to follow the Sun as it moves across the sky! Almost every day, heavy rainstorms drench the canopy.

Only a few giant trees poke higher than the top of the canopy.

Some of the animals living in the canopy never come down to the ground.

One of the biggest and slowest leaf eaters in the canopy is the sloth. To save energy, it sleeps 16 hours a day!

Life in a Rain Forest

Mossy Branches

In the moist canopy, mosses and algae coat every branch and even grow on some of the leaves. However, some canopy leaves have smooth, waxy surfaces that are too slippery for mosses and algae to attach themselves.

THE SECRET WORLD OF A BROMELIAD

Bromeliads are **epiphytes**—plants that rest on the branches of trees and hang their roots in the air. A bromeliad plant is a busy place! Many insects hide beneath its leaves, so lizards and birds often stop by looking for a tasty meal. In the center of the leaves is a tiny pool of rainwater, where insect larvae (young) and tadpoles often live.

A Room at the Top

The huge branches of rain forest trees are also home to epiphytes. These plants grow high up from the ground and collect moisture by dangling their roots in the damp air. One such plant, called a bromeliad, channels rain into a central cup with its upward-pointing, overlapping leaves.

Epiphytes draw their **nutrients** from the rotting remains of algae, mosses, and leaves.

The Forest Strangler

The strangler fig starts life as an epiphyte in the canopy but sends its roots down the trunk of the tree it lives on to the forest floor. Eventually, the fig blocks out all the tree's light. By the time the tree dies, the fig's thick roots have formed a new trunk.

Life in a Rain Forest

Fruity Business

The highest trees in the forest spread their light seeds in the wind, but for the shorter trees wind-power is not an option. Lower down, where the air is still, trees produce seeds inside sweet, juicy fruits. These tempt fruit-eating bats, birds, and monkeys. Large seeds are coughed up, often some distance from the parent tree. Small seeds pass right through an animal's digestive system. The seeds then sprout from the animal's droppings, which provide a rich, ready-made **fertilizer!**

More than 30 million species of insects live in the world's rain forests.

Fruit bats love to feast on sugary fruit. They find food during the day, using their senses of smell and sight.

Life in the Canopy

This katydid looks like it is from outer space, but it is a type of grasshopper! It eats leaves and small insects.

Leaf Munchers

For many insects and some large **mammals**, the leaves of the canopy are an endless supply of food. Even though some of the leaves are poisonous, most leaf eaters can eat the poisoned leaves of the tree they live on. Some insects even use the poison to their advantage. They store it in their bodies to keep predators from eating them.

Say It with Flowers

Before they can make seeds and fruit, trees and other plants need to be **fertilized**. This occurs when **pollen**, a fine yellow powder made by flowers, is carried from one flower to another of the same **species**. Animals, especially insects, act as pollen carriers. They are attracted to flowers by **nectar**, a sweet and highly nutritious liquid. As the animals sip the nectar, pollen grains brush onto them. When they go on to visit another flower of the same species, they fertilize it accidentally.

The passion vine climbs up trees of the forest. Its flowers' bright petals attract animal visitors.

A hummingbird hovers in midair, sipping nectar from a flower. The tiniest of birds, some hummingbirds are no bigger than a large bee.

Hummingbirds are the only birds in the world that can fly backward.

Big Bird

Of all the rain forest's animals, birds are the best suited to life in the treetops. There are more species of birds in tropical South America than anywhere else in the world. Not all birds drink nectar. Many eat insects, lizards, and small mammals. Right at the top of the canopy's food chain are the harpy eagles, the largest birds in the forest. They are powerful birds that eat animals as big as monkeys and sloths. Harpy eagles swoop silently down to snatch up their **prey** in their razor-sharp talons.

Life in the Canopy

All Kinds of Noises

The forest canopy is a noisy place. It is so densely packed with leaves and branches that animals cannot see very far. Instead, many forest animals use sound to communicate with others of their own species. In the forest canopy, the air is thick with screeches, howls, rattles, grunts, croaks, and clicks.

Howler monkeys are the noisiest of all the animals in the rain forest. Their calls can travel as far as 2 miles (3.2 km) across the rain forest.

> The South American douroucouli is the only nocturnal, or night, monkey in the world.

THE FOOD CHAIN

Food chains show how living things depend on one another. Plants are at the start of the chain. They make their own food from sunlight and water. Plant eaters are animals such as sloths that eat leaves, fruit, or nectar. Plant eaters are eaten by carnivores (animals that eat other animals), which are the next step in the chain.

plants   plant eaters   carnivores

Life in a Rain Forest

A PREHENSILE TAIL

A tail that can grasp is called **prehensile**. Many animals of the South American rain forest have prehensile tails, including monkeys, opossums, climbing porcupines, and anteaters. Prehensile tails give an animal five limbs to climb with. The animal can anchor itself firmly to a branch with its tail, leaving its hands free to pick at fruit or insects.

Tree frogs have sticky suction pads on their toes to hold on to slippery branches.

Moving Around

The animals of the canopy are specially suited to life in the trees. Many insects, lizards, and mammals have sharp claws that grip the rough bark. Frogs use their sticky feet to cling to tree branches.

Monkeys are the champion climbers of the rain forest. They travel far in search of their favorite food, fruit, and rarely come down to the ground. Monkeys can grab branches with their hands, feet, or tails. Some species can leap across gaps of 30 feet (9 m).

Only monkeys from South and Central America can grip with their tails.

Understory Life

In the understory, the hanging roots of figs dangle in midair, while lianas and creeping vines coil upward. Only a little light filters through the canopy, so plants there have to make the most of it. Palms and tree ferns have huge leaves, which can be up to 3 feet (0.9 m) long. Animals climb up and down the lianas or swing on the vines.

The see-through wings of glasswing butterflies make them almost invisible in the tree shade.

Many kinds of snakes slink through the understory of the forest.

The branchless trunks of canopy trees tower up toward the light.

The tamandua's long, snouty nose is perfect for thrusting into a nest to suck up a tasty termite meal.

Home Breaker

The tamandua, or lesser anteater, is always searching for a meal. Tamanduas live mainly on termites, antlike insects that can be found all over the rain forest. Termites build rock-hard nests on the sides of trees. Tamanduas have huge, sharp claws that they use to break into these insect fortresses. The animals' spiky tongues dart in and out of the hole they make, slurping up insects as they go.

When feeding, tamanduas can thrust their tongues in and out of a termite's nest at a rate of 160 strokes a minute!

Understory Life

LIANAS: LADDERS IN THE FOREST

Lianas are woody plants that rely on trees for support. They cling to saplings, or young trees, on the forest floor and grow with them until they reach the canopy. Lianas live longer than many trees, and when their host tree dies, they often start climbing up another tree. For many climbing mammals, such as the squirrel monkey (inset, below), lianas act as ladders between the forest floor and the canopy!

Life in a Rain Forest

Prowling Predators

Birds fly beneath the canopy, safe from eagles patrolling the skies. Many birds raise their young there, too, nesting inside rotten tree trunks. The hope of a tasty, defenseless meal brings **predators** such as monkeys and hawks down from the treetops. Snakes, weasels, and coatis (small mammals) venture up from the forest floor in search of eggs and chicks.

Snakes are among the quietest animals that hunt in the understory. They slither noiselessly upon their prey. The mottled colors of their bodies blend in with tree bark.

This chestnut-mandibled toucan uses its long, curved beak to pick and eat fruit and small animals.

Understory Life

A COLORFUL WORLD

Many rain forest animals are brightly colored. Poisonous frogs and insects are often blue, red, or yellow. The bright colors warn other animals not to eat them. Some harmless animals copy these colors, so that they won't be eaten either! Many birds have bright colors that blend with the leaves, flowers, and trees of the forest. That way they can remain unseen by their enemies.

Hidden Cats

Small cats such as the ocelot, the jaguarundi, and the margay prey on small birds, mice, and lizards. Jaguars take bigger prey. They are well **camouflaged**, with spotted yellow and black coats that seem to disappear in the dappled sunlight.

Life on the Forest Floor

Little light reaches the forest floor, so few plants grow there. The rotting piles of leaves make an ideal home for insects and fungi. Beneath the **leaf litter,** the soil is thin and poor in nutrients, so the trees do not put down deep roots. Instead, they send their roots along or just beneath the ground, sucking nutrients from the rotting leaves.

The horned frog looks very much like the leaf litter of the forest floor.

Rain forest tarantulas grow to more than 3 inches (7.6 cm) long. They eat insects, mice, and sometimes small birds!

The floor of the rain forest is covered with soft piles of decaying leaves.

Rain forest trees are supported by giant buttress roots that grow out from their trunks.

The Fight for Light

Many rain forest trees produce large seeds, with enough food inside for their saplings to reach 3 feet (0.9 m) or more. Once this food runs out, a sapling sits in the shade for years, hardly growing. It must wait until a tall tree dies and falls, opening up space in the canopy.

What's for Dinner?

The shortage of plant life on the forest floor means that many animals live off what falls down from the branches above. Beetles, termites, and other insects eat leaf litter and wood. These animals in turn are eaten by larger insects, spiders, lizards, and mammals.

In the rain forest, leaves can rot away completely within a week of falling to the ground.

Life on the Forest Floor

Armies of Ants

Ants are the most successful insects of the forest floor. There are many different species, but they all live and work together in communities that are thousands strong.

Columns of army ants, armed with painful stings and powerful jaws, march across the forest floor, devouring nearly everything in their path. Many forest birds take advantage of the chaos the ants cause, following close behind the columns of ants and picking off the insects they disturb.

> A column of army ants can contain more than 20 million insects.

LEAF-CUTTERS

Leaf-cutters are the champion weight lifters of the ant world. Every day, they cut segments from canopy leaves and carry them all the way down to their underground nests. Leaf-cutter ants can lift leaf segments that are more than 50 times their own weight! They do not eat the leaves they collect. Instead, they chew them up and spit them out as mulch. They live on a fungus that grows on the mulch.

Life in a Rain Forest

Mammals of the Forest Floor

One of the most common mammals of the forest floor is the agouti. This rabbit-sized rodent has a plentiful supply of Brazil nuts all to itself. No other animal can bite through the hard shells of the nuts. The agouti hides its Brazil nuts in underground stores and then digs them up when food is scarce. Sometimes it forgets where it has hidden its secret larder, and a few of the seeds sprout.

Only about 5 percent of sunlight reaches the floor of the rain forest.

The agouti is the only animal in the rain forest with a strong enough bite to break a Brazil nutshell.

> Tapirs are shy plant eaters. They are hunted by jaguars and forest people.

Tapirs and Hunters

At more than 6 feet (1.8 m) long, the tapir is one of the largest animals in the forest. Its long snout ends in a short trunk. The tapir eats leaves, shoots, and buds. It likes to feed near streams, rivers, and lakes. A good swimmer, the tapir can escape into the water if a predator appears.

The most dangerous animals of the forest floor are jaguars and snakes. But people hunt there, too. Native peoples use poison blow darts to shoot down birds and monkeys from the branches.

> Three of the four species of tapirs in the world live in the rain forests of South America. The other species lives in Malaysia.

Life in a Tree Near You

The trees in your neighborhood are full of life, too, like the trees of a rain forest. Look out for birds hopping from branch to branch, searching for fruit, berries, insects, and grubs. They raise their families in trees as well, either in nests, hidden among the leaves, or in hollowed-out holes in the trunk of the tree.

Like a toucan, the woodpecker builds a nest and raises its young inside a tree's trunk.

Pet cats are related to the ocelots and jaguars of the rain forest. They are also predators.

TOP TIPS FOR NATURE WATCHERS

1 Keep a birding diary. Note when you see birds flying to your tree with twigs and grasses for their nests or food for their chicks.

2 Put out food, such as seeds and nuts, to attract birds to your garden. Make sure the food is well out of reach of any cats.

3 In icy weather, put out a bowl of water. Birds can drink and bathe there when water everywhere else has frozen over.

Nesting Boxes

If you have a garden with a tree in it, why not ask your parents to put up a nesting box? If some birds lay their eggs in it, you will be able to watch the parent birds as they fly back and forth, carrying food for their growing chicks.

In fall, you may see squirrels leaping nimbly from branch to branch in search of nuts for winter storage. There is always plenty of life to see in every tree. All you have to do is look!

Life in a Rain Forest

Glossary

camouflaged: when an animal has colors and patterns that help it blend in with its surroundings

epiphytes: plants that dangle their roots in the air

fertilized: when male parts of a plant or animal have joined with the female parts to produce new plants or animals

fertilizer: manure or chemicals that make soil richer in nutrients

leaf litter: decaying leaves

mammals: warm-blooded, hairy animals that feed their young milk

nectar: a sweet sugar-water made by plants to tempt animals

nutrients: plant food, found in soil and leaf litter

pollen: yellow powder made by the male part of a flower

predators: animals that hunt other animals for food

prehensile: able to grip; many forest animals have a prehensile tail

prey: an animal that is eaten by another animal

species: a group of closely related animals, plants, or other living things

Index

agouti 6, 28
ant 27
butterfly 5, 6, 7, 18
epiphyte 10, 11
food chain 15
frog 7, 17, 23, 24
fruit 12, 13
fruit bat 12
harpy eagle 6, 14

hummingbird 14
jaguar 6, 7, 23, 29
katydid 13
liana 18, 21
leaf litter 24, 26
monkey 6, 7, 12, 14, 15, 16, 17, 21, 22, 29
peccary 6, 7
poison 13, 23, 29

seed 8, 12, 13, 26, 28, 31
sloth 6, 9, 14, 15
snake 5, 6, 7, 19, 22, 29
strangler fig 6, 11, 18
tamandua 6, 20
tapir 7, 29
tarantula 25
termite 20, 26
toucan 6, 22